HAMLET

HAMLET
By William Shakespeare

Adapted by
Kathleen Thompson and Michael Nowak
Illustrated by Fran Balistreri

RSVP
RAINTREE
STECK·VAUGHN
PUBLISHERS
The Steck-Vaughn Company

Austin, Texas

Library of Congress Number: 88-27446

Library of Congress Cataloging-in-Publication Data

Thompson, Kathleen.
  Hamlet / Kathleen Thompson and Michael Nowak; illustrated by Francis Balistreri.

  SUMMARY: Hamlet, the prince of Denmark, is urged by his father's ghost to avenge his murder by his wife and his brother who has seized the throne.
  [1. Princes—Fiction. 2. Murder—Fiction 3. Revenge—Fiction.]
  I. Thompson, Kathleen. II.Balistreri, Francis, ill. III. Title.
  PZ7.G4817Ham   [Fic.]—dc19   1988   88-27446

ISBN 0-8172-2764-4 hardcover library binding

ISBN 0-8114-6825-9 softcover binding

15 14 13 12   07 06 05

Cast of Characters

Claudius, King of Denmark

Hamlet, nephew to the king

Polonius, counselor to the king

Horatio, friend of *Hamlet*

Laertes, son to *Polonius*

Courtiers: *Voltemand, Cornelius, Rosencrantz, Guildenstern, Osric*

Soldiers: *Marcellus, Bernardo, Francisco*

Reynaldo, servant to *Polonius*

Fortinbras, Prince of Norway

Players, two clowns, grave diggers, a Norwegian captain, English ambassadors

Gertrude, mother to *Hamlet*, Queen of Denmark

Ophelia, daughter to *Polonius*

Ghost of Hamlet's father

HAMLET, PRINCE OF DENMARK
ACT I
Scene 1

The scene is a platform where guards keep watch in front of Elsinore castle in Denmark. The guards have recently seen a ghost that looked like the dead King Hamlet. One of them, BERNARDO, is waiting for two friends of the young Prince Hamlet, HORATIO and MARCELLUS. They enter.

BERNARDO. Welcome, Horatio. Welcome, good Marcellus.

MARCELLUS. What, has this thing appeared again tonight?

BERNARDO. I have seen nothing.

MARCELLUS. Horatio says 'tis but our fantasy.
Therefore, I have invited him along
With us to watch the minutes of this night;
That if again this ghostly form should come,
He may believe our eyes and speak to it.
(The GHOST *enters.)* Peace, break thee off; look, where it comes again!

BERNARDO. In the same figure, like the king that's dead.

MARCELLUS. Thou art a scholar; question it, Horatio.

HORATIO. (To GHOST) What art thou that steals that fair and warlike form
In which the majesty of buried Denmark
Did sometimes march?

MARCELLUS. It is offended.

BERNARDO. See, it stalks away!

HORATIO. Stay! Speak, speak! I charge thee, speak!

(Cock crows.)

MARCELLUS. Shall I strike at it?

HORATIO. Do, if it will not stand.

BERNARDO. 'Tis here!

HORATIO. 'Tis here!

MARCELLUS. 'Tis gone! *(The GHOST leaves.)*

BERNARDO. It was about to speak, when the cock crowed.

HORATIO. And then it started like a guilty thing.
But look, the morn, in russet mantle clad,
Walks o'er the dew of yon high eastward hill:
Let us go tell what we have seen tonight
Unto young Hamlet; for, upon my life,
This spirit, dumb to us, will speak to him

Scene 2

A public room in the castle. The new king, CLAUDIUS, enters with the queen, GERTRUDE. GERTRUDE is PRINCE HAMLET's mother, but almost as soon as his father, KING HAMLET died, she married the new king, his brother. The KING and QUEEN are followed by PRINCE HAMLET, who has come back from college in Wittenberg for his father's funeral and his mother's wedding. They are also followed by POLONIUS, the king's adviser, and his son, LAERTES, as well as a number of other Lords and attendants.

KING. Though yet of Hamlet our dear brother's death
The memory be green, and though it well became us
To bear our hearts in grief,
We join that with remembrance of ourselves.
Therefore we have our recent sister, now our queen,

Taken to wife. And you have freely gone
With this affair along. For all, our thanks.
And now, Laertes, what's the news with you?
You told us of some suit. What wouldst thou have?

LAERTES. Your leave and favor to return to France.

KING. Have you your father's leave? What says Polonius?

POLONIUS. He hath, my lord, wrung from me my slow leave.

KING. Take thy fair hour, Laertes. Time be thine.
But now, my nephew Hamlet, and my son —
How is it that the clouds still hang on you?

HAMLET. Not so, my lord; I am too much in the sun.

QUEEN. Good Hamlet, cast thy nighted color off.
Do not forever with thy vailed lids
Seek for thy noble father in the dust.
Thou must know 'tis common. All that lives must die,
Passing through nature to eternity.
Why seems it so particular with thee?

HAMLET. Seems, madam! Nay, it is. I know not 'seems.'
Tis not alone my inky cloak, good mother,
Together with all forms, moods, shapes of grief,
That may describe me truly. These indeed seem,
For they are actions that a man might play.
But I have that within which passeth show —
These but the trappings and the suits of woe.

KING. 'Tis sweet and approvable in your nature, Hamlet,
To give these mourning duties to your father.
But, you must know, your father lost a father.
That father lost, lost his. We pray you, throw to earth
This most uncommon woe, and think of us as of a father.

QUEEN. I pray thee, stay with us. Go not to Wittenberg.

HAMLET. I shall in all my best obey you, madam.

KING. Why, 'tis a noble and a fair reply.

(All except HAMLET leave. He stays behind and speaks his
thoughts out loud.)

HAMLET. O God! O God!
How weary, stale, flat and unprofitable,
Seem to me all the uses of this world.
Fie on it! Ah, fie! That it should come to this!
But two months dead — nay, not so much, not two —
So excellent a king, so loving to my mother!
Frailty, thy name is woman!
A little month, before those shoes were old
With which she followed my poor father's body —
Why she, even she — married with my uncle.
My father's brother, but no more like my father
Than I to Hercules. O, most wicked speed!
But break, my heart, for I must hold my tongue.

(HORATIO, MARCELLUS, and BERNARDO enter.)

HORATIO. Hail to your lordship!

HAMLET. I am glad to see you well, my friend.
And what make you from Wittenberg, Horatio?
And what is your affair in Elsinore?

HORATIO. My lord, I came to see your father's funeral.

HAMLET. I pray thee, do not mock me, fellow-student.
I think it was to see my mother's wedding.

HORATIO. Indeed, my lord, it followed close upon.

HAMLET. Thrift, thrift, Horatio! The funeral baked meats
Did coldly furnish forth the marriage tables.
My father! Methinks I see my father.

HORATIO. Where, my lord?!

HAMLET. In my mind's eye, Horatio.

HORATIO. I saw him once. He was a goodly king.

HAMLET. He was a man, take him for all in all.
I shall not look upon his like again.

HORATIO. My lord, I think I saw him yesternight.

HAMLET. Saw? Who?

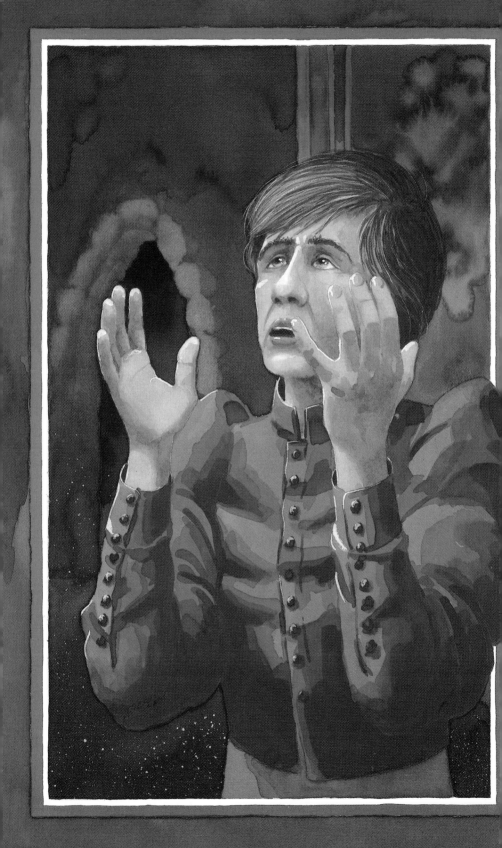

HORATIO. My lord, the king your father.

HAMLET. The king my father!

HORATIO. Two nights together had these gentlemen,
Marcellus and Bernardo, on their watch,
In the dead vast and middle of the night
Been thus encountered. A figure like your father
Appears before them, and with solemn march
Goes slow and stately by them. This to me
In deepest secrecy they did express.
And I, with them, the third night kept the watch.

HAMLET. But where was this?

MARCELLUS. My lord, upon the platform where we watched.

HAMLET. Did you not speak to it?

HORATIO. My lord, I did.
But answer made it none.

HAMLET. Hold you the watch tonight?

MARCELLUS. We do, my lord.

HAMLET. I will watch tonight. Perchance 'twill walk again.

Scene 3

A room in Polonius' house. His son, LAERTES, is preparing to leave for school in France. OPHELIA is Polonius' daughter, and she and Hamlet are in love with each other. POLONIUS enters, full of hypocritical advice for his son.

POLONIUS. Yet here, Laertes! Aboard, aboard, for shame!
For you are waited for. My blessing with thee
And this advice take in thy memory.
My son, be friendly, but by no means common.
Those friends thou hast, of proven loyalty,
Grapple them to thy soul with hoops of steel;

11

But do not waste your gold with entertainment
Of each new-hatched, unfledged comrade. Beware
Of entrance to a quarrel, but being in,
Fight so that thy opponent may beware of thee.
Give every man they ear, but few thy voice.
Neither a borrower nor a lender be,
For loan oft loses both itself and friend.
This above all: to thine own self be true,
And it must follow, as the night the day,
Thou canst not then be false to any man.

LAERTES. Most humbly do I take my leave, my lord.
Farewell, Ophelia, and remember well
What I have said to you.

OPHELIA. 'Tis in my memory locked.

(LAERTES *leaves.*)

POLONIUS. What is it, Ophelia, he hath said to you?

OPHELIA. So please you, something touching the Lord
Hamlet.

POLONIUS. What is between you? Give me up the truth.

OPHELIA. He hath, my lord, of late made many tenders
Of his affection to me.

POLONIUS. Do not believe his vows. I would not, in
plain terms, from this time forth have you so slander
any moment leisure as to give words or talk with the
Lord Hamlet.

OPHELIA. I shall obey, my lord.

Scene 4

The guard platform just before midnight. The air bites
shrewdly. It is very cold.

HORATIO. It is a nipping and an eager air.

HAMLET. What hour now?

HORATIO. I think it lacks of twelve.

MARCELLUS. No, it is struck.

HORATIO. Indeed? I heard it not. Then it draws near the
Season wherein the spirit has been seen to walk.
Look, my lord, it comes! (*Enter GHOST.*)

HAMLET. Angels and ministers of grace defend us!
Be though a spirit of health or goblin damned,
Thou comest in such questionable shape
That I will speak to thee. I'll call thee Hamlet,
King, father, royal Dane. O, answer me!

HORATIO. It beckons you to go away with it.

HAMLET. It will not speak. Then, I will follow it.

HORATIO. Do not, my lord.

HAMLET. Why, what should be the fear?
I do not set my life at a pin's price.
It waves me forth again. I'll follow it.

Scene 5

Another part of the platform.

HAMLET. Where wilt thou lead me? Speak. I'll go no further.

GHOST. I am thy father's spirit,
Doomed for a certain time to walk the night.
If thou didst ever thy dear father love —
Revenge his foul and most unnatural murder.

HAMLET. Murder!

GHOST. Murder most foul, as in the best it is;
But this most foul, strange and unnatural.
The serpent that did sting thy father's life
Now wears his crown.

HAMLET. O my prophetic soul! My uncle!

GHOST. Brief let me be. Sleeping within my orchard,
My custom always of the afternoon,
Upon my secure hour thy uncle stole,
With juice of cursed hebenon in a vial
And in the opening of my ear did pour the poison.
Thus was I, sleeping, by a brother's hand
Of life, of crown, of queen, at once made free.
O, horrible! O, horrible! most horrible!
If thou hast nature in thee, bear it not.
Adieu, adieu! Hamlet, remember me.

HAMLET. O all you host of heaven! O earth, what else!
O villain, villain, smiling damned villain!
O, one may smile, and smile, and be a villain.
At least I'm sure it may be so in Denmark.

(Enter HORATIO and MARCELLUS)

HAMLET. Never make known what you have seen tonight.

HORATIO. O day and night, but this is wonderous strange!

HAMLET. There are more things in heaven and earth,
    Horatio,
Than are dreamt of in your philosophy.
But come, never, however strange or odd I bear
Myself — as I perhaps hereafter shall think well
To act a foolish and a witless part —
Then never let them see that you know what I do.
The time is out of joint. O cursed spite,
That ever I was born to set it right!

ACT II
Scene 1

A room in Polonius' house. POLONIUS has just sent a spy to check on his son, LAERTES, when OPHELIA enters. She has just been with HAMLET, who is pretending to be mad.

POLONIUS. How now, Ophelia! What's the matter?

OPHELIA. My lord, as I was sewing in my chamber,
Lord Hamlet, with his jacket all a mess;
No hat upon his head; pale as his shirt;
As if he had been loosed out of hell
To speak of horrors — he comes before me.

POLONIUS. Mad for thy love?

OPHELIA. My lord, I do not know;
But truly, I do fear it.

POLONIUS. Have you given him any hard words of late?

OPHELIA. No, my good lord, but, as you did command,
I did refuse his letters and would not
Allow him in my company.

POLONIUS. It's made him mad. Come, go we to the king.

Scene 2

A room in the castle. The KING and QUEEN and POLONIOUS enter.

POLONIUS. I will be brief. Your noble son is mad.
That he is mad, 'tis true. 'Tis true 'tis pity,
And pity 'tis, 'tis true: a foolish figure.
Mad let us grant him, then. And now remains
That we find out the cause of this effect.
I have a daughter — have while she is mine —
Hath given me this. (*Reads from a letter.*)
"Doubt thou the stars are fire;
Doubt that the sun doth move
Doubt truth to be a liar;
But never doubt I love.
Thine evermore, most dear lady, HAMLET."

KING. But how hath she received his love?

POLONIUS. She took the fruits of my advice, and he,
Rejected, fell into the madness wherein now he raves.

KING. How may we try it further?

POLONIUS. You know, sometimes he walks here in the
lobby.
At such a time, I'll send my daughter to him.
Be you and I behind a curtain then.
Mark the encounter.

KING. We will try it.

QUEEN. But, look, where sadly the poor wretch comes
reading.

POLONIUS. Away, I do beseech you, both away.

(*The* KING *and* QUEEN *leave.* HAMLET *enters, reading.*)

POLONIUS. What do you read, my lord?

HAMLET. Words, words, words.

POLONIUS. What is the matter, my lord?

HAMLET. Between who?

POLONIUS. I mean the matter that you read, my lord.

HAMLET. Lies, sir. For the rogue says here that old men have gray beards, that their faces are wrinkled, and that they have a plentiful lack of wit. All of which I most powerfully believe, but I do not think it honest to have set it down. For you, yourself, sir, should be as old as I am, if like a crab you could go backwards.

POLONIUS. *(Aside)* Though this be madness, yet there is method in it. (To HAMLET) My honorable lord, I will most humbly take my leave of you.

HAMLET. You cannot, sir, take from me anything that I will more willingly part with — except my life, except my life, except my life.

(POLONIUS leaves and ROSENCRANTZ and GUILDENSTERN enter. They are two old friends of Hamlet's, sent by the KING and QUEEN to find out what is going on with him.)

GUILDENSTERN. My honored lord!

ROSENCRANTZ. My most dear lord!

HAMLET. What have you, my good friends, deserved at the hands of fortune, that she sends you here to prison?

GUILDENSTERN. Prison, my lord?

HAMLET. Denmark's a prison

ROSENCRANTZ. We think not so, my lord.

HAMLET. Why, then, 'tis none for you. For there is nothing either good or bad but thinking makes it so. To me it is a prison. But let me ask you, by the rights of our fellowship, whether you were sent for or no? If you love me, do not hold back.

GUILDENSTERN. My lord, we were sent for.

HAMLET. I will tell you why. I have of late — but wherefore I know not — lost all my mirth. This goodly frame, the earth, seems to me a sterile island. This most excellent canopy, the air, appears to me a foul concentration of

vapors. What a piece of work is a man! How noble in reason! in action how like an angel! in understanding how like a god! And yet, to me, what is this dust? Man delights me not. No, nor woman neither, though by your smiling you seem to say so.

ROSENCRANTZ. My lord, there was no such stuff in my thoughts.

HAMLET. Why did you laugh then, when I said "man delights me not"?

ROSENCRANTZ. To think, my lord what poor entertainment, then, the players shall receive from you. Hither are they coming to offer you service.

(PLAYERS *enter, with* POLONIUS.)

HAMLET. You are welcome, masters. I am glad to see you well. Come, give us a taste of your quality. Come, a passionate speech.

FIRST PLAYER. What speech, my lord?

HAMLET. I heard thee speak me a speech once, but it was never acted. Or if it was, not above once. For the play, I remember, pleased not the million. One speech in it I chiefly loved. It speaks of Hecuba when she sees her husband's body dead.

FIRST PLAYER. "Who this had seen,
    'Gainst Fortune's state would treason have pronounced.
    But if the gods themselves did see her then,
    Unless things mortal move them not at all,
    Would have made flow the burning eyes of heaven,
    And passion in the gods."

POLONIUS. Look, whether he has not turned his color and has tears in his eyes. Pray you no more.

HAMLET. 'Tis well. I'll have thee speak out the rest soon. Good my lord, Polonius, will you see the players well lodged? Take them in.

(POLONIUS leaves with ROSENCRANTZ, GUILDENSTERN and all the players except the FIRST.)

HAMLET. Can you play the Murder of Gonzago?

FIRST PLAYER. Ay, my lord.

HAMLET. We'll have it tomorrow night. You could study a speech of some dozen lines, which I would set down and insert in it, could you not?

FIRST PLAYER. Ay, my lord.

HAMLET. Very well. Follow that lord.

(The FIRST PLAYER leaves. HAMLET, alone, speaks his thoughts.

HAMLET. Oh, what a rogue and peasant slave am I.
Is it not monstrous that his player here,
But in a fiction, in a dream of passion,
Could force his soul so to imagining
That from her working all his face grew pale?
And all for nothing. All for Hecuba!
What's Hecuba to him, or he to Hecuba,
That he should weep for her? What would he do
Had he the reason and the cue for passion
That I have? He would drown the stage with tears.
Yet I, I can say nothing. This is most brave,
That I, the son of a dear father murdered,
Prompted to my revenge by heaven and hell,
Must now unpack my heart with words!
Fie upon it. About, my brain! I have heard
That guilty creatures sitting at a play
Have, by the scene, been struck so to the soul
That they proclaim their evil deeds.
I'll have these players here play something like
The murder of my father for mine uncle.
And I will watch his looks. If he but pale,
I'll know my course. The play's the thing
Wherein I'll catch the conscience of the king.

Act III

Scene 1

A room in the castle. The KING and POLONIUS, who have called for HAMLET, wait with OPHELIA.

POLONIUS. Ophelia, walk you here. Read on this book.
I hear him coming: let's withdraw, my lord.

(The KING and POLONIUS hide. HAMLET enters.)

HAMLET. To be, or not to be: that is the question:
Whether 'tis nobler in the mind to suffer
The slings and arrows of outrageous fortune,
Or to take arms against a sea of troubles,
And by opposing end them? To die, to sleep;
To sleep: perchance to dream: ay, there's the rub;
For in that sleep of death what dreams may come
Must give us pause.
For who would bear the whips and scorns of time,
To grunt and sweat under a weary life,
But that the dread of something after death,
It makes us rather bear those ills we have
Than fly to others that we know not of?
Soft you now! The fair Ophelia!

OPHELIA. Good my lord,
How does your honor for this many a day?

HAMLET. I humbly thank you; well, well, well.

OPHELIA. My lord, I have remembrances of yours,
That I have longed to re-deliver;
I pray you, now receive them.

HAMLET. I did love you once.

24

OPHELIA. Indeed, my lord, you made me believe so.

HAMLET. You should not have believed me. I loved you not.

OPHELIA. I was in love then fooled.

HAMLET. Get thee to a nunnery: why wouldst thou be a breeder of sinners? Get thee to a nunnery, go. Or, if thou wilt marry, marry a fool. For wise men know well enough what monsters you make of them. To a nunnery, go, and quickly too. Farewell. *(He leaves.)*

OPHELIA. O, what a noble mind is here overthrown!

(The KING and POLONIUS come out of hiding.)

KING. Love! His affections do not that way tend.
And what he spoke, though it lacked form a little,
Was not like madness. But there's danger here.
He shall with speed to England. It shall be so.
Madness in great ones must not unwatched go.

Scene 2

A grand hall in the castle. HAMLET and HORATIO enter. HAMLET tells his friend to watch the KING's face during the play. The KING and QUEEN enter amid much ceremony, attended by POLONIUS, OPHELIA, ROSENCRANTZ, GUILDENSTERN and attendants.

QUEEN. Come hither, my dear Hamlet, sit by me.

HAMLET. No, good mother, here's metal more attractive.

(Two PLAYERS enter, PLAYER KING and PLAYER QUEEN.)

P. KING. Thirty dozen moons about the world have been
Since love our hearts united in most sacred bands.

P. QUEEN. So many journeys may the sun and moon
Make us again ere love be done!

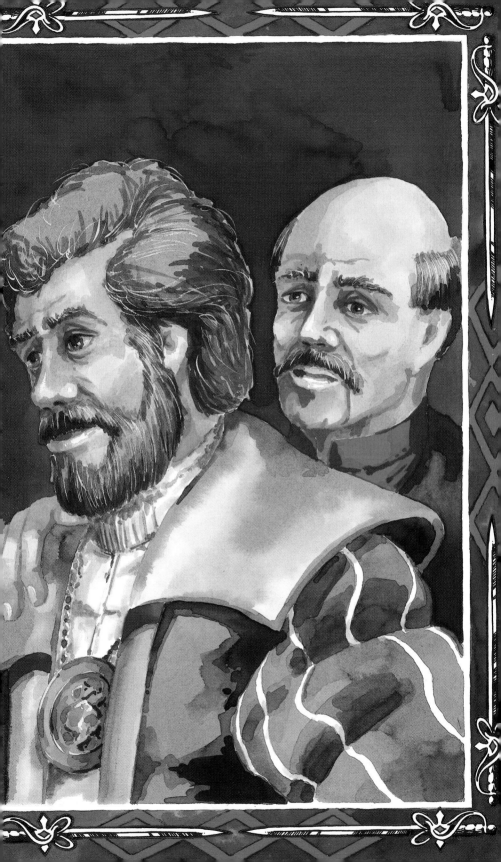

P. KING. 'Tis deeply sworn. Sweet, leave me here awhile. My spirits grow dull.

(The PLAYER KING goes to sleep.)

HAMLET. Madam, how like you this play?

QUEEN. The lady doth protest too much, methinks.

KING. What do you call the play?

HAMLET. *The Mousetrap.* This is one Lucianus, nephew to the king.

(Another PLAYER pours poison in the PLAYER KING's ear.)

HAMLET. He poisons him in the garden for his estate. His name is Gonzago. You shall see how the murderer gets the love of Gonzago's wife.

OPHELIA. The king rises!

HAMLET. What, frightened by false fire!

QUEEN. How fares my lord?

KING. Give me some light: away!

ALL. Lights, lights, lights!

(Everyone leaves except HAMLET and HORATIO.)

HAMLET. O good Horatio, I'll take the ghost's word for a thousand pounds. Did you see?

HORATIO. Very well, my lord.

(POLONIUS re-enters.)

POLONIUS. My lord, the queen would speak with you and presently.

HAMLET. I will come to my mother by and by.

POLONIUS. I will say so.

HAMLET. By and by is easily said. Leave me, friends.

(HORATIO and POLONIUS leave.)

'Tis now the very witching time of night,
When churchyards yawn and hell itself breathes out
Infection to this world. Now could I do
Such bitter business as the day
Would quake to look on. Soft! Now to my mother.
I will speak daggers to her, but use none.

Scene 3

A room in the castle. The KING and POLONIUS enter.

POLONIUS. My lord, he's going to his mother's room:
Behind the curtain I will hide myself,
To hear them speak.
I'll call upon you ere you go to bed,
And tell you what I know.

KING. Thanks, dear my lord.

(*POLONIUS leaves.*)

O, God, my crime is foul, it smells to heaven.
A brother's murder! What if this cursed hand
Were thicker than itself with brother's blood,
Is there not rain enough in the sweet heavens
To wash it white as snow?
O wretched state! O bosom black as death!

(*The KING kneels and begins to pray. At that moment, HAMLET enters and pulls out his sword. The KING does not see him.*)

HAMLET. Now might I do it well, now he is praying;
And now I'll do't. (*Stops.*) And so he goes to heaven.
A villain kills my father, and for that,
I, his sole son, do this same villain send
To heaven? No!
When he is drunk asleep, or in his rage,
At gaming, swearing, or about some act
That has no flavor of salvation in it,

Then trip him, that his heels may kick at heaven,
And that his soul may be as damned and black
As hell, whereto it goes.

(HAMLET *leaves, and the* KING *rises.)*

KING. My words fly up, my thoughts remain below:
Words without thoughts never to heaven go.

Scene 4

The QUEEN's room. The QUEEN waits HAMLET. POLONIUS is hidden behind a curtain. HAMLET enters.

HAMLET. Now, mother, what's the matter?

QUEEN. Hamlet, thou hast thy father much offended.

HAMLET. Mother, you have my father much offended.

QUEEN. Have you forgot me?

HAMLET. Come, come, and sit you down. You shall not budge.
You go not till I set you up a mirror
Where you may see the inmost part of you.

QUEEN. What wilt thou do? Thou wilt not murder me?
Help, help, ho!

POLONIUS. (Behind curtain.) What, ho! help, help, help!

HAMLET. How now! A rat? Dead, for a ducat, dead!

(HAMLET *thrusts his sword through the curtain and stabs* POLONIUS.)

POLONIUS. O, I am slain! (*He falls and dies.*)

QUEEN. O me, what hast thou done?

HAMLET. Is it the king?

(*He lifts the curtain and discovers* POLONIUS's *body.*)

Thou wretched, interfering fool, farewell!
I thought you were your better.
(To his mother) Peace! Sit you down!

QUEEN. What have I done, that thou darest wag thy tongue
In noise so rude against me?

HAMLET. Look here, upon this picture of two brothers.
See, what a grace was seated on this brow,
Where every god did seem to set his seal.
This was your husband. Look you now what follows:
Here is your husband now. Like a mildewed ear.
Then what judgement would step from this to this?
O Shame! Where is thy blush?

QUEEN. O, speak to me no more;
These words like daggers, enter in mine ears;
No more, sweet Hamlet!

(The GHOST of HAMLET's father enters. HAMLET can see the GHOST, but the QUEEN cannot.)

HAMLET. You heavenly guards! What would your gracious figure?

QUEEN. Alas, he's mad!

GHOST. Do not forget: this visit is
To sharpen thy most nearly blunted purpose.
But, look, amazement on thy mother sits.
Speak to her, Hamlet.

HAMLET. How is it with you, lady?

QUEEN. Alas, how is't with you?
To whom do you speak this?

HAMLET. Do you see nothing there?

QUEEN. Nothing at all; yet all there is I see.

HAMLET. Why, look you there! look how it steals away!
My father, in his habit as he lived!

(The GHOST leaves.)

Confess yourself to heaven;
Repent what's past. Avoid what is to come.

QUEEN. O Hamlet, thou hast torn my heart in two.

HAMLET. O, throw away the worser part of it,
And live the purer with the other half.
Good night, but go not to mine uncle's bed.

ACT IV
Scene 1

A room in the castle. The KING and QUEEN enter.

QUEEN. Ah, mine own lord, what have I seen tonight!

KING. What, Gertrude? How does Hamlet?

QUEEN. Mad as the sea and wind;
Behind the curtain hearing something stir,
Whips out his rapier, cries, "A rat, a rat!"
And kills the unseen good old Polonius.

KING. O heavy deed! Where is he gone?

QUEEN. To take away the body he hath kill'd.

KING. O, come away!
My soul is full of discord and dismay.

Scene 2

Another room in the castle. HAMLET enters.

HAMLET. Safely stowed.

ROSENCRANTZ and GUILDENSTERN *(Outside)* Hamlet! Lord Hamlet!

HAMLET. But soft, what noise? who calls on Hamlet?

(ROSENCRANTZ and GUILDENSTERN enter.)

ROSENCRANTZ. My lord, you must tell us where the body is and go with us to the king.

HAMLET. The body is with the king, but the king is not with the body. The king is a thing —

GUILDENSTERN. A thing, my lord!

HAMLET. Of nothing: bring me to him. Hide fox, and all after.

(*HAMLET runs away and the two chase after him.*)

Scene 3

Another room in the castle. The KING enters with his attendants.

KING. I have sent to seek him, and to find the body. How dangerous is it that this man goes loose!

(*HAMLET, ROSENCRANTZ, and GUILDENSTERN enter.*)

KING. Now, Hamlet, where's Polonius?

HAMLET. At supper.

KING. At supper! Where?

HAMLET. Not where he eats, but where he is eaten.

KING. Alas, alas! Where is Polonius?

HAMLET. In heaven. Send thither to see. If your messenger find him not there, seek him in the other place yourself. But indeed, if you find him not within this month, you shall smell him as you go up the stairs into the lobby.

KING. (*To his attendants.*) Go seek him there.

HAMLET. He will stay till you come.

KING. Hamlet, this deed must send thee hence. Therefore prepare thyself for England.

(*HAMLET, ROSENCRANTZ and GUILDENSTERN leave.*)

And, England, if my love thou hold'st at all,
Thou mayst not coldly see our royal wish —
Which we send thee in letters with his friends —
The present death of Hamlet. Do it, England.

Scene 4

Elsinore. A room in the castle. The QUEEN enters, followed by OPHELIA, who has gone mad and covered her clothing with wildflowers.

OPHELIA. Where is the beautiful majesty of Denmark?

QUEEN. How now, Ophelia!

OPHELIA. Say you? Nay, pray you, mark.
   (She sings.) He is dead and gone, lady,
   He is dead and gone;
   At his head a grass-green turf,
   At his heels a stone.

   (The KING enters.)

QUEEN. Alas, look here, my lord.

KING. How do you, pretty lady?

OPHELIA. Well, God shield you! They say the owl was a baker's daughter. Lord, we know what we are, but know not what we may be. God be at your table!

KING. How long hath she been thus?

OPHELIA. I hope all will be well. We must be patient; but I cannot choose but weep, to think they should lay him i' the cold ground. My brother shall know of it: and so I thank you for your good counsel. Come, my coach! Good night, ladies; good night, sweet ladies; good night, good night. *(She leaves.)*

KING. O, this is the poison of deep grief; it springs
  All from her father's death.

QUEEN. Alack, what noise is this?

(There is a loud noise as LAERTES *enters, followed by a crowd of Danes.)*

LAERTES. O thou vile king, where is my father?

KING. Dead.

QUEEN. But not by him.

LAERTES. How came he dead? I'll be revenged for him.

KING. I am guiltless of your father's death,
  And am most thoroughly in grief for it.

LAERTES. How now! What noise is that?

*(*OPHELIA *re-enters.* LAERTES *sees in moment that she is mad.)*

O heavens! is't possible, a young maid's wits
Should be as mortal as an old man's life?

OPHELIA. *(Sings.)* And will he not come again?
  And will he not come again?
  No, no, he is dead:
  Go to thy death-bed:
  He never will come again. *(She leaves.)*

LAERTES. Do you see this, O God?

KING. Make choice of whom your wisest friend you will,
  And they shall hear and judge 'twixt you and me.
  And where the crime is let the great axe fall.
  I pray you, go with me.

Scene 5

Another part of the castle. HORATIO is reading a letter from HAMLET, brought by a SAILOR, standing by.

HORATIO. *(Reads.)* "Horatio, before we were two days old

at sea, a pirate's ship gave us chase. Finding ourselves too slow of sail, we were forced to fight, and in the grapple I boarded them. On the instant they got clear of our ship, so I alone became their prisoner. They have dealt with me like thieves of mercy. This good fellow will bring thee where I am. Rosencrantz and Guildenstern hold their course for England. Of them I have much to tell thee. Farewell. Hamlet." (*To* SAILOR) Direct me to him from whom you brought this letter.

Scene 6

Another room in the castle. The KING and LAERTES enter. HAMLET has returned to Denmark and the KING and LAERTES have made a plot to kill him. The KING will bet that HAMLET can beat LAERTES in a fencing match and LAERTES will tip his sword with a fatal poison. In case that doesn't work, the KING will have a cup of wine poisoned and trick HAMLET into drinking it when he is thirsty from the match. The QUEEN enters.

QUEEN. One woe doth tread upon another's heel,
So fast they follow. Your sister's drown'd, Laertes.

LAERTES. Drown'd! O, where?

QUEEN. There is a willow grows near to a brook,
There with fantastic flowers did she come and fall.
Her clothes spread wide and for a while they held her
Up, Which time she chanted snatches of old tunes.
But long it could not be until her dampened clothes
Pull'd the poor wretch to muddy death.

LAERTES. Too much of water hast thou, poor Ophelia,
And therefore I forbid my tears. Adieu, my lord.
(*He leaves.*)

KING. How much I had to do to calm his rage!
Now fear I this will give it start again;
Therefore let's follow.

39

ACT V
Scene 1

A churchyard. Two grave diggers enter with spades and other tools. They talk as they work.

GRAVE DIGGER 1. What is he that builds stronger than either the mason, the shipwright, or the carpenter?

(*HAMLET and HORATIO enter, but they are not seen by the grave diggers.*)

Batter thy brains no more about it, and, when you are asked this question next, say "a grave-maker." The houses that he makes last till doomsday. Go, fetch me a cup of liquor.

(*The second grave digger leaves. The first grave digger sings while he digs.*)

HAMLET. Has this fellow no feeling of his business, that he sings at grave-making? I will speak to him. Whose grave is this, sirrah?

GRAVE DIGGER 1. Mine, sir.

HAMLET. I think it be thine, indeed, for thou liest in it.

GRAVE DIGGER 1. You lie out of it, sir, and therefore it is not yours. For my part, I do not lie in it, and yet it is mine.

HAMLET. What man dost thou dig it for?

GRAVE DIGGER 1. For no man, sir.

HAMLET. What woman, then?

GRAVE DIGGER 1. For none, neither.

HAMLET. Who is to be buried in it?

GRAVE DIGGER 1. One that was a woman, sir. But, rest her soul, she's dead. And newly dead. Here's a skull now has lain in the earth three and twenty years.

HAMLET. Whose was it?

GRAVE DIGGER 1. This same skull, sir, was Yorick's skull, the king's jester.

HAMLET. Let me see. Alas, poor Yorick! I knew him, Horatio. He hath carried me on his back a thousand times. Where be your jokes now? Your songs? Your flashes of laughter that used to set the table on a roar?

(A large procession enters. It is led by priests, followed by attendants carrying the corpse of OPHELIA. Following the body are LAERTES, the KING and QUEEN, and other attendants.)

The queen, the courtiers: who is this they follow?
Hide we awhile, and mark.

(HAMLET and HORATIO go off to the side to watch.)

LAERTES. Lay her in the earth:
And from her fair and unpolluted flesh
May violets spring!

HAMLET. What, the fair Ophelia!

QUEEN. Sweets to the sweet: farewell!

(She scatters flowers on the grave.)

I hoped thou shouldst have been my Hamlet's wife.
I thought thy bride-bed to have deck'd, sweet maid,
And not have strewed thy grave.

LAERTES. Hold off the earth awhile,
Till I have caught her once more in mine arms.

(LAERTES leaps into the grave. HAMLET steps out of hiding.)

HAMLET. What is he whose grief bears such an emphasis?
This is I, Hamlet the Dane. *(He leaps into the grave.)*

LAERTES. The devil take thy soul! (*He grabs* HAMLET.)

HAMLET. Thou pray'st not well.
I pray thee, take thy fingers from my throat.

KING. Pull them apart.

(*Some attendants separate* HAMLET *and* LAERTES.)

HAMLET. I loved Ophelia. Forty thousand brothers
Could not, with all their quantity of love,
Make up my sum. (*To* LAERTES)What is the reason that
You use me thus? I loved you ever. (*He storms out.*)

KING. Horatio, go after him.

Scene 2

A hall in the castle. HAMLET and HORATIO enter. HAMLET has told HORATIO about discovering that the KING planned for him to be killed in England. He has also accepted the challenge to duel with LAERTES.

HORATIO. You will lose this contest, my lord.

HAMLET. I do not think so. But thou wouldst not think how ill all's here about my heart: but it is no matter.

HORATIO. If your mind dislike something, obey it. I will say you are not fit.

HAMLET. No. The hand of God is even in the fall of a sparrow. If it be now, 'tis not to come. If it be not to come, it will be now. If it be not now, yet it will come. The readiness is all.

(*The* KING *and* QUEEN *enter, followed by* LAERTES *and attendants.*)

KING. Come, Hamlet, come, and take this hand from me.

(*The* KING *puts* LAERTES' *hand into* HAMLET'*s.*)

HAMLET. Give me your pardon, sir. I've done you wrong,
But pardon it, as you are a gentleman.

LAERTES. I do receive your offered love like love,
And will not wrong it.

HAMLET. I embrace it freely. Give us the swords.

LAERTES. *(Looking at a sword)* This is too heavy, let me see
another. *(He switches one of the swords for one with a poisoned
tip.* HAMLET *does not notice.)*

HAMLET. Come on, sir.

LAERTES. Come, my lord.

(They begin fight. HAMLET *touches* LAERTES *with his sword and
the judge calls it a hit.)*

KING. Stay; give me drink. Here's to thy health. *(He tries
to get* HAMLET *to drink.)* Give him the cup.

HAMLET. I'll play this round first. Come.

*(*HAMLET *and* LAERTES *begin again. And again* HAMLET *touches*
LAERTES *with his sword.)*

LAERTES. A touch, a touch, I do confess.

QUEEN. *(Picking up the poisoned cup.)* The queen carouses
to thy fortune, Hamlet.

KING. Gertrude, do not drink.

QUEEN. I will, my lord. I pray you, pardon me. *(She drinks.)*

(When HAMLET *isn't looking,* LAERTES *stabs him with the sword.*
HAMLET, *angered, furiously fights with* LAERTES. *While they
are fighting, their swords are exchanged. Then* HAMLET *stabs*
LAERTES *with the poisoned sword.)*

KING. Part them!

(The QUEEN *falls.)*

HORATIO. They bleed on both sides.

LAERTES. I am justly killed with mine own treachery.

HAMLET. How does the queen?

KING. She faints to see them bleed.

QUEEN. No, no, the drink, the drink! O my dear Hamlet!
The drink, the drink! I am poisoned. (*She dies.*)

HAMLET. O villany! Treachery! Seek it out.

LAERTES. It is here, Hamlet. Hamlet, thou art slain;
The treacherous instrument is in thy hand.
Thy mother's poisoned. The king, the king's to blame.

HAMLET. The point is poisoned too!
Then, poison, to thy work.

(*He stabs the KING with the poisoned sword.*)

Here, thou treacherous, murderous, damned Dane,
Follow my mother.

(*The KING dies.*)

LAERTES. Exchange forgiveness with me, noble Hamlet.
Mine and my father's death come not upon thee,
Nor thine on me! (*He dies.*)

HAMLET. Heaven make thee free of it! I follow thee.
I am dead, Horatio. Report me and my cause aright
To the unsatisfied. O, I die, Horatio.
The rest is silence. (*He dies.*)

HORATIO. Good night, sweet prince,
And flights of angels sing thee to thy rest!

GLOSSARY

adieu   (ə dyü′) the French word for "good bye"

ducat   (də′ kət) a coin, usually made of gold, that was once used in a number of European countries

hebenon   (heb′ ə nən) a word that means "poisonous plant," however, hebenon is not a real plant

Hecuba   (hek′ yü bə) in the *Iliad,* by Homer, the wife of Priam

hither   (hith′ ər) to this place

mantle   (man′ tel) a loose piece of sleeveless clothing that is worn over other clothing, usually regarded as a symbol of authority

perchance   (pər chans′) perhaps; possibly

prophetic   (prō fet′ ik) relating to prophecy, or the foretelling of events

shipwright   (ship′ rīt) a carpenter that builds or repairs ships

villainy   (vil′ ə nē) the state of being an evil or vile character

'twixt   (twikst) a short form of *betwixt,* which means "between"